SOUTH WEST ENGLAND ENGLAND BUSES: 1990 TO 2005

SOUTH WEST ENGLAND BUSES: 1990 TO 2005

DAVID MOTH

AMBERLEY

First published 2018

Amberley Publishing
The Hill, Stroud
Gloucestershire, GL5 4EP

www.amberley-books.com

Copyright © David Moth, 2018

The right of David Moth to be identified as
the Author of this work has been asserted in
accordance with the Copyrights, Designs and
Patents Act 1988.

ISBN 978 1 4456 8605 9 (print)
ISBN 978 1 4456 8606 6 (ebook)

British Library Cataloguing in Publication Data.
A catalogue record for this book is available from
the British Library.

Origination by Amberley Publishing.
Printed in the UK.

Introduction

Welcome to this collection of images of buses in the South West of England. Unlike my previous books, in which all photographs were taken by me, for this volume I have included several taken and submitted by Robert Appleton and Matthew Wharmby.

Between the three of us, hopefully we have managed to include something of interest for all followers of the bus scene in this corner of England. The one area that is probably conspicuous by its absence is the north coast of Devon; I just simply never got round to going there. I still haven't to be honest, although I do intend to, at some point.

It is a matter of regret that I didn't get down to Cornwall before 2002 to record the remaining Bristol VRTs still in service with First there. I think it was simply a matter of not being able to do it as a day trip from Essex or Cambridgeshire, unlike say Bristol or Salisbury, so it was a trip that needed some planning. But I'm glad I did make the effort as it was like stepping back in time to see so many VRTs still in normal service, albeit in more contemporary liveries than I was used to seeing them in.

I am also sorry to say that Plymouth Citybus is very much under-represented. I only made one trip to Plymouth, in May 2004, and my interest at the time was in the remaining Bristol VRTs still in service with First.

I did make several trips to Bristol and Bath and took loads of photographs of Badgerline buses in service there in their very attractive livery of green and yellow. I was also drawn to Bristol by the colourful Cityline fleet and their strictly enforced policy at the time of allocating specific vehicle types to each route. Of course, Cityline became part of the Badgerline Group when Badgerline purchased its parent company, Midland Red West, in 1988.

I visited Swindon in August 1995 and found the bus scene there fascinating, as there were both the council-owned Thamesdown Transport, with its Fleetlines and Dominators, and Swindon & District, which was part of Cheltenham & Gloucester, whose parent company, Western Travel, had been taken over by Stagecoach in 1993 and was in the throes of being updated and repainted. I promised myself at the time that I would return to Swindon soon, but somehow almost twenty-three years have passed and I never did get round to going back there. Of course, Thamesdown Transport is now part of the Go-Ahead Group, as is Wilts & Dorset, who bucked the trend of most former NBC companies by remaining independent until August 1993.

I visited Salisbury and the Bournemouth area more times than I can remember between 1991 and 2004, and as a result there are loads of W&D and Yellow Buses photographs in this book.

There are plenty of Southern National and Smiths photographs as well, taken in Dorset. Southern Vectis is represented by only one image, as they are covered in my book *South East England Buses in the 1990s*.

The photographs in this book are arranged in a rough west to east order, starting with a VRT in Land's End and finishing with two VRTs in Lymington bus station.

I have never worked in the bus industry, so it is probably inevitable that I may have got the occasional fact wrong, for which I can only apologise.

Compiling the images of this book has certainly brought back lovely memories of trips to this pleasant part of England and the interesting varieties of vehicle types and liveries.

I would like to take this opportunity to thank both Robert Appleton and Matthew Wharmby for their help, both in submitting images for the book and also for their encouragement.

I must also mention Rob Sly's wonderful website in providing information regarding the history of several Bristol VRTs and REs, which can be found at http://bcv.robsly.com/.

Finally, my thanks to Connor Stait of Amberley Publishing for his continual advice and encouragement.

David Moth
April 2018

First Devon &Cornwall Bristol VRT AJF 706T stands in a commemorative Western National livery at Land's End on Tuesday 11 June 2002.

First Devon & Cornwall Bristol VRT 1224 (LFJ 871W) is seen on layover at Penzance on 11 June 2002.

4422 (M422 CCV), a First Devon & Cornwall Dennis Dart with Plaxton Pointer bodywork, is seen in Penzance on Tuesday 11 June 2002.

First Devon & Cornwall Dennis Dart 4410 (M410 CCV) is captured at St Ives on 11 June 2002.

Bristol VRT AJF 753T was new to Western National as 1151 in 1979. It had a spell with Nottingham Omnibus and Ryan of Bath in the 1990s before returning to Cornwall in 1996, where it spent several years in service with Truronian. It is seen in England's southernmost settlement, Lizard, in Cornwall, on Saturday 31 May 2003.

First Devon & Cornwall Bristol VRT 1253 (TWS 915T) was new to Bristol in 1979 as 5134. It is seen in Falmouth on 31 May 2003 with what seems to be a slight mismatch in the livery on the lower front dash panel with the rest of the bus.

First Devon & Cornwall Mercedes 0709D 6670 (H345 LJN) was new to Thamesway in 1991 as 336. It is seen here on a local service in Truro on 25 March 2003.

Also seen in Truro on 25 March 2003 is Dennis Dart 4417 (M417 CCV), which was new to Western National in 1995.

First Devon & Cornwall coach-seated Leyland Olympian 1754 (A754 XAF) is seen at Pentire Head, just outside Newquay, on 10 June 2002. Later renumbered 34754, this bus is now preserved.

Also at Pentire Head on 10 June 2002 is Western Greyhound Mercedes 0814D S501 SRL.

First Devon & Cornwall 1978 Bristol VRT 1134 (AFJ 699T) is seen in Newquay bus station about to head off to Truro on the scenic 89A via Perranporth on 10 June 2002. Later renumbered 38699, this bus is believed to survive in Spain.

Also taken in Newquay on 10 June 2002 was this image of two Bristol VRTs: 1257 (PWY 38W) on the left and 1134 (AFJ 699T) on the right. PWY 38W was withdrawn by First in 2004 and is believed to survive in Belgium.

New to South Wales Transport in 1979 as 961, Bristol VRT 1134 (WTH 961T) is seen in Newquay bus station on 10 June 2002. Being renumbered 38661 before being withdrawn by First in 2005, this bus is now preserved in South Wales NBC red.

First Bristol VRT 1143 (AJF 743T) is seen passing Par railway station en route to Truro on the 24A on 26 March 2003. It was interesting to note how many route variations requiring suffix letters there were at the time on First's network in Cornwall.

New to Western National as 1176 in 1980, First Devon & Cornwall Bristol VRT 38808 (FDV 808V) is seen on Monday 10 May 2004 in Plymouth bus station, about to depart on the very lengthy and very scenic 81B via the Torpoint ferry to Cremyll on the Rame Peninsula. This bus was withdrawn and scrapped in 2005.

Also seen in Plymouth on 10 May 2004 is Bristol VRT 38846 (LFJ 846W). New to Western National as 1202 in 1980, this bus was withdrawn in 2006, and at the time of writing is owned by the British Women Racing Drivers' Club, Silverstone.

Plymouth Citybus Dennis Dart/Plaxton 33 (T133 EFJ) is seen on Monday 10 May 2004.

Badgerline Volvo B10M/Alexander 112 (D112 GHY) is seen in Taunton, setting out on the lengthy 102 to Weston-super-Mare, on 23 June 1992. (Photograph copyright: Robert Appleton)

Southern National Leyland Leopard 282 (DAD 257T) is also seen in Taunton on 23 June 1992. This coach was new to National Travel South East in 1979 and spent some time with the Brutonian fleet. (Photograph copyright: Robert Appleton)

Southern National Leyland Leopard/Plaxton 2439 (LOD 720P) also spent some time in the Brutonian fleet, and is also seen in Taunton on 23 June 1992. (Photograph copyright: Robert Appleton)

Southern National Bristol LH/Plaxton Supreme III 3307 (AFJ 727T), new to Western National, is seen in Minehead on Tuesday 23 June 1992. This vehicle is now preserved in NBC green dual-purpose livery with Western National fleet names. (Photograph copyright: Robert Appleton)

Bridgwater depot, photographed on 23 June 1992. Southern National was sold to its management in March 1988, but when photographed Bridgwater depot still displayed NBC signage. (Photograph copyright: Robert Appleton)

Badgerline Bristol RE 1297 (EHU 391K) is seen arriving at Glastonbury on 28 August 1991. Since I took this photograph the road layout at this location has changed, and a residential development was built at this junction in 2011.

Bristol RE EHU 391K is seen in Glastonbury town centre on 28 August 1991.

Badgerline open-top Bristol VRT 8619 (AHW 114P) is seen in Weston-super-Mare on Monday 22 June 1992. (Photograph copyright: Robert Appleton)

New in May 1987, Badgerline Volvo B10M Citybus/Alexander 5706 (D706 GHY) later passed into the ownership of First Group, who later converted it to an open-top bus, working in Cornwall. 22 June 1992. (Photograph copyright: Robert Appleton)

Badgerline Mercedes/Optare 0811D 3800 (E800 MOU) is seen in Wells on Saturday 20 June 1992. (Photograph copyright: Robert Appleton)

Also seen in Wells on 20 June 1992 is Badgerline Leyland Lynx 3610 (H610 YTC). (Photograph copyright: Robert Appleton)

Another bus seen in Wells on Saturday 20 June 1992 is Badgerline Bristol RE 1302 (HHW 915L). (Photograph copyright: Robert Appleton)

Badgerline Leyland National 3079 (YFB 970V), seen on Saturday 25 June 1992. This bus saw further service with Northern Bus of Dinnington and MTL Manchester. (Photograph copyright: Robert Appleton)

Cityline Bristol VRT 5136 (AHU 513V) is seen in Gloucester Road North, Filton, Bristol, on 25 April 1991.

Cityline Bristol VRT 5108 (PHY 702S) is seen in Bristol city centre on 4 October 1993 with an Olympian and a Lynx in the background. The Olympian would have been a matter of months old at the time.

Cityline Leyland Olympian/Roe 9505 (JHU 904X) is seen resting at the Avonmouth terminus of the cross-Bristol 42 from Park Estate on Thursday 25 April 1991. At the time Cityline had a policy of allocating specific vehicle types to specific routes, which is something they had in common with London Buses.

Cityline Leyland Olympian/Northern Counties 9603 (K603 LAE) is seen when just a few months old at the Hartcliffe terminus of the cross-Bristol 77 on Monday 4 October 1993. This batch of Olympians had recently ousted elderly dual-door Bristol VRTs from this group of routes.

Cityline Leyland Lynx 1648 (H648 YHT) is seen when only a few months old on a slightly dull day in Filton on the cross-Bristol 3 to Broomhill. This busy service combined with the 1 and 2 to provide eight buses an hour from the city centre to Broomhill. Thursday 25 April 1991.

Here we see Leyland Lynx 1648 (H648 YHT) a couple of years later in the late afternoon sunshine of Friday 2 September 1993, waiting to depart on its long and busy journey on the cross-Bristol 1 to Broomhill.

In the 1990s, Dennis Darts with boxy Plaxton Pointer bodywork became a common sight in bus fleets throughout Britain. This style of body was also fitted to Volvo B6s. Cityline Dennis Dart 1538 (M538 FFB) is seen at Temple Meads station on the 8 to Clifton. The young woman in this photograph is a friend of mine. Wednesday 16 March 2000.

Cityline Leyland Olympian 9549 (A949 SAE) is captured in Bristol city centre on Sunday 21 June 1992. (Photograph copyright: Robert Appleton)

Above and below: Although normal operation of Bristol Lodekkas by Bristol ceased in 1984, Bristol and its successor Cityline kept on Bristol FLF C7262 (GAE 883D) in semi-preservation, and it worked a peak hours-only diagram most working days for several years until withdrawal in December 1993. It is seen here on Monday 4 October 1993, about to depart on the cross-Bristol 1 to Broomhill.

Cityline Bristol FLF C7262 (GAE 883D) is seen again at the Broomhill terminus of the 1, 2 and 3 group of routes in the early evening of 4 October 1993, about to head to Southmead on the 2.

In this photograph, GAE 883D is seen at the University of the West of England in Bristol, having worked a morning peak service from the city centre on the morning of 4 October 1993. This bus was exported to Germany soon after withdrawal and was believed to have been destroyed. However, it was rediscovered in 2014 and is under restoration in Germany at the time of writing.

Cityline Leyland National 1460 (OAE 758R) is seen on loan to Badgerline, working a Bath city service on Thursday 25 June 1992. (Photograph copyright: Robert Appleton)

Cityline Bristol VRT 5102 (PHY 696S) is seen on the 75 to Hartcliffe on Sunday 21 June 1992. Not long after this the VRTs were ousted from this route by new Leyland Olympians. (Photograph copyright: Robert Appleton)

Cityline Bristol VRT 5114 (RHT 508S) is seen in Bristol city centre on 21 June 1993. (Photograph copyright: Robert Appleton)

Cityline Bristol VRT 5140 (AHU 517V) is also seen in Bristol city centre on Sunday 21 June 1992. (Photograph copyright: Robert Appleton)

Cityline Leyland Lynx 1605 (F605 RTC) is captured in Bristol city centre, again on 21 June 1992. (Photograph copyright: Robert Appleton)

Also seen in Bristol city centre on 21 June 1992 is Cityline Leyland Lynx 1607 (F607 RTC). (Photograph copyright: Robert Appleton)

Badgerline Leyland Olympian 9006 (G906 TWS) is about to enter Bristol bus station when seen here on the afternoon of Friday 2 September 1994.

Badgerline Bristol VRT 5517 (PEU 512R) has just left Bristol bus station when captured here on 2 September 1994.

Badgerline Bristol VRT 5564 (XHK 224X) was new to Eastern National in 1981 as 3119. It passed to Thamesway upon the partitioning of Eastern National in 1990 and was transferred to Badgerline in 1991. It is seen departing Bristol bus station on Saturday 27 June 1992. It is interesting to note the nonstandard application of the Badgerline fleet name between the decks. (Photograph copyright: Robert Appleton)

Another former Eastern National/Thamesway Bristol VRT is 5553 (KOO 791V), seen departing Bristol bus station on 27 June 1992 on the 309 to Dursley. (Photograph copyright: Robert Appleton)

Badgerline Leyland National 2 3604 (A204 YWP) is snapped leaving Bristol bus station on Saturday 27 June 1992. (Photograph copyright: Robert Appleton)

Badgerline Leyland Olympian/Roe 8614 (A814 THW), in an updated version of the livery, complete with an oversized badger, is seen in Bristol, also on 27 June 1992. (Photograph copyright: Robert Appleton)

Above and below: Both Badgerline Bristol VRT 5067 (MOU 741R) and Badgerline Leyland Olympian 9002 (A902 TWS) are seen departing Bristol bus station on 27 June 1992, with the latter working service X39 to Bath. (Photograph copyright: Robert Appleton)

Badgerline Leyland Olympian 9508 (JHU 907X) is also seen in Bristol. (Photograph copyright: Robert Appleton)

Seen in Bristol, also on 27 June 1992, is Badgerline Leyland Olympian 9516 (LWS 532Y). (Photograph copyright: Robert Appleton)

A Badgerline Dennis Lance with Plaxton Verde bodywork, 129 (L129 TFB) is seen in the environs of Bristol bus station, about to work the lengthy 308 to Gloucester via Thornbury on Friday 2 September 1994.

Cityline Volvo Olympian/Northern Counties Palatine 2 9671 (S617 AAE) is seen in First 'Barbie' livery in central Bristol. This bus was later renumbered 34171 under the First national renumbering scheme and was transferred to Taunton. Wednesday 16 March 2000.

Badgerline Metrobus 6004 (DAE 514W) is seen entering Bath bus station on Thursday 25 April 1991.

Similarly, Badgerline Metrobus 6002 (DAE 512W) is also seen in Bath on Thursday 25 June 1992. (Photograph copyright: Robert Appleton)

Above and below: When I took these pictures there weren't many Bristol VRTs left in service with Badgerline. 5534 (EWS7 42W) is seen on University service 18 in Bath on Friday 17 March 2000. Note that by this time the Badgerline fleet name had been relegated to the sides of the bus to make way for the more prominent First logo.

Badgerline open-top Bristol VRT 8607 (UFX 859S) is seen on the Bath Tour on Thursday 25 June 1992.

One of only three S-reg Bristol VRTs delivered new to Eastern National, 5562 (UVX 2S), which had a Leyland 510 engine, is seen on a local Bath service. This was one of several VRTs that passed to Thamesway in 1990, which, finding themselves no longer required, were transferred within the Badgerline Group to the Badgerline fleet in early 1991. 25 June 1992.

First Badgerline Dennis Trident/East Lancs Lolyne 9713 (W713 RHT) is captured working on the Bath Park and Ride service on 27 September 2000.

On the same day, 9713 is seen in Bath city centre in the company of First Badgerline Dennis Dart/ Plaxton Pointer L218 VHU. This was during the period when the First Group were gradually phasing out the traditional (and not so traditional) local company names.

Badgerline Leyland National 2 3519 (AAE 663V) is seen in Bath, working one of the less direct routes to Bristol on Thursday 25 June 1992. This bus would have been new to Bristol during the NBC era. (Photograph copyright: Robert Appleton)

South Wales Transport Bristol VRT 974 (BEP 974V) is captured in Bath while on loan to Badgerline, presumably in connection with the Glastonbury Festival. 25 June 1992. (Photograph copyright: Robert Appleton)

Badgerline Bristol VRT 8600 (RTH 931S) *I. K. BRUNEL* was new to South Wales Transport. It is seen here in Bath after having been transferred to the Badgerline fleet. Although carrying a livery for the Bath Tour, it is seen working on Bath local service 14A on Thursday 25 June 1992. (Photograph copyright: Robert Appleton)

Badgerline Bristol VRT 8601 (RTH 932S) *Wm. HERSCHEL* was also new to South Wales Transport and, like its sister 8600, is seen on local route 14A on 25 June 1992. This bus is of course named after the astronomer William Herschel who, in his garden in Bath, in 1781, while searching for undiscovered comets, discovered the planet that would be named Uranus after the Roman god who was Saturn's father. Herschel himself wasn't in favour of the name, however: his preference was to call it George's Star after the reigning king of England. (Photograph copyright: Robert Appleton)

Badgerline convertible Bristol VRT 8606 (VDV 137S) *MINERVA* is seen sans roof working on the Bath Tour on 25 June 1992. (Photograph copyright: Robert Appleton)

We see 8606 a few years later on 17 March 2000 in a revised version of the Bath Tour livery. This time with its roof in place, it is working on the University route 18. My friend appears in an image for a second time, with her consent.

Badgerline Leyland Olympian 8611 (A811 THW) is seen in Bath, followed by a Rover SD1, on 25 June 1992. (Photograph copyright: Robert Appleton)

Badgerline coach-seated all-Leyland Olympian 9010 (G910 TWS) looks great from the rear in the attractive Badgerline livery when caught at Bath bus station on 25 June 1992. (Photograph copyright: Robert Appleton)

Badgerline Bristol VRT 5545 (EWS 753W) is seen in Chippenham on Friday 2 September 1994.

Bristol VRT 5551 (KOO 792V) looks every inch a native Badgerline bus despite her Essex heritage. One of ten midlife Bristol VRTs transferred from Thamesway to Badgerline in 1991, these differed from the indigenous Badgerline VRTs in only having seventy seats instead of seventy-four. KOO 792 was new to Eastern National as 3074. It is seen on 25 April 1991 on layover in Bath bus station.

Another former Eastern National/Thamesway Bristol VRT that was transferred to Badgerline was STW 33W. New to Eastern National as 3089, it is seen here near the Clifton Suspension Bridge, now numbered 5560 in the Badgerline fleet, on the 358 to Portishead. At the time of writing it is looking likely that Portishead may have its railway service restored in the not too distant future. 2 September 1993.

Badgerline 5509 (KOU 795P) is a very early series 3 Bristol VRT and is seen on layover at Chippenham bus station. Note the BRISTOL VR badge on the grille. In the late '70s the National Bus Company stipulated that it didn't wish for new deliveries to have this badge, although they continued to be fitted on new VRTs for other operators who ordered them.

Badgerline Bristol VRT 5537 is seen sideways on in the attractive north Wiltshire town of Devizes. It has just arrived from Chippenham and will soon be returning on the scenic 233. Friday 2 September 1994.

Badgerline Bristol VRT 5509 (EWS 744W) is departing Chippenham on the 233 to Devizes. 2 September 1994.

Cottrell's MCW Metrobus Mk 1 GBU 2V (new to Greater Manchester Buses) is seen in Cinderford on the wet morning of Saturday 3 September 1994. As was not unusual with small independent operators at the time, no route number is displayed.

Another view of GBU 2V taken on 3 September 1994. This time it is seen at lunchtime in Gloucester, heading back out to Cinderford. The weather has not improved.

Red & White was a former NBC company that was part of the Western Travel Group. The Western Travel Group was taken over by Stagecoach in 1993, although it did take quite a while for a lot of the buses in the various fleets of Western Travel to receive Stagecoach stripes. Leyland Olympian 828 (A548 HAC) is still wearing Red & White livery when seen in Gloucester on Saturday 3 September 1994.

This Cheltenham & Gloucester Bristol VRT (EWS 751W) is still wearing the very attractive Stroud Valleys mint green and yellow livery when seen here in Stroud on 3 September 1994. This bus is preserved in Stagecoach 'rolling ball' livery.

Just a matter of months old at the time, Stagecoach Gloucester City Bus Volvo B6 833 (L833 CDG) is seen at Brockworth on Saturday 3 September 1994.

Stagecoach Gloucester Citybus Volvo B6 836 (L836 CDG) is seen caught in early afternoon traffic in Gloucester on 3 September 1994.

Above and below: Two views of Midland Red West Dennis Lance/Plaxton Verde 255 (M255 MRW), seen when nearly new at the unmistakable location of Gloucester bus station. The Dennis Lance with Plaxton bodywork was the closest thing there was to a standard type of bus for the Badgerline Group. These photographs were taken not long after the formation of FirstBus from the merger of the Badgerline and GRT groups. A 'Welcome to FirstBus' window etching can be seen in the front nearside window of the bus. Friday 11 August 1995.

Cheltenham & Gloucester's parent company Western Travel was taken over by Stagecoach in November 1993. But not unusually for a Stagecoach acquisition in the 1990s, it took some time to repaint the fleet, especially the older types. On 11 August 1994, Bristol VRT 229 (EWS 746W) is captured loading in Stroud for a rural run out to Tetbury, still in the attractive mint green Stroud Valleys livery. This bus was later transferred to Stagecoach Hampshire Bus.

Also on Friday 11 August 1995 Stagecoach Stroud Valleys Bristol VRT 227 (EWS 740W) is reversing out of the bay at Gloucester bus station, about to head to Forest Green via Stroud on the very scenic 93. It is still in the attractive mint green livery, although is beginning to look in need of a repaint, which it did receive, albeit into Stagecoach Stripes. Unlike a lot of people I personally thought that the Stagecoach Stripes liveries actually suited the classic ECW body quite well.

Hampshire Bus was purchased directly from the NBC in April 1987 by Stagecoach holdings as part of the NBC privatisation process. The Leyland Olympian with Alexander bodywork was the standard Stagecoach Group double-decker for several years in the late 1980s and early '90s. 211 (G211 SSL) is seen at the old Amesbury bus station on the 8, which was operated jointly with Wilts & Dorset. This bus was later renumbered 14961 and relocated to Gloucester. 19 April 1993.

Former GM Buses Leyland Titan GNF 11V in service with Stagecoach Swindon & District in Swindon. This was one of very few Titans that were originally built with one door. 11 August 1995.

An attractive BET style Safeway Leyland Leopard, PYC 746L, new in 1973, is seen in Yeovil on Monday 15 June 1991. (Photograph copyright: Robert Appleton)

Safeway's Leyland Leopard/Willowbrook RYA 676L, seen in Yeovil bus station on Friday 26 June 1992, was also new in 1973. (Photograph copyright: Robert Appleton)

Safeway Services Leyland Leopard/Duple Dominant TYD 911W in Yeovil, again on Friday 26 June 1992. This bus is now preserved. (Photograph copyright: Robert Appleton)

VPF 42M, a Willowbrook-bodied Leyland Leopard, is also seen in Yeovil bus station on Friday 26 June 1992. It had been new to Safeguard, Guildford, in 1974 and was acquired by Safeway in 1982. (Photograph copyright: Robert Appleton)

Southern National Bristol VRT AFJ 764T is seen on the Isle of Portland on Wednesday 12 May 1993. This bus is now preserved in NBC green.

Southern National Leyland Olympian UWW 9X and Smith's RE YHY 586J are seen in Southwell, Isle of Portland, on 12 May 1993. The Olympian was new to West Yorkshire PTE in 1982. This batch of Olympians found their way into several fleets throughout England after withdrawal by West Yorkshire PTE.

Southern National Bristol VRT AFJ 765T is seen resting at Southern National's Weymouth depot on Saturday 12 August 1995.

Southern National Leyland Olympian 1804 (A680 KDV) is seen here at King's Statue on the Weymouth seafront. New to Devon General, this Olympian was one of the last batch of chassis built by Bristol Commercial Vehicles upon closure in 1983. 12 August 1995.

Southern National convertible Bristol VRT 934 (VDV 134S) stands at Axminster railway station with a friend of mine in the image on 12 May 1993.

Southern National convertible Bristol VRT 934 (VDV 134S), with the station building of Axminster railway station in the background, is also seen on 12 May 1993.

Southern National Bristol VRT VDV 134S is seen at Weymouth on Saturday 12 August 1995, this time without its roof.

One last image of Southern National Bristol VRT 934 (VDV 134S), taken on 12 August 1995. This bus has since been preserved in a version of Southern National livery.

Smiths Bristol RE YHY 586J, seen at Southwell, Isle of Portland, on 12 May 1993. She was new to Bristol.

Smiths Bristol RE YHY 586J is seen again on a much sunnier day, 12 August 1995, at Weymouth's King's Statue.

Smiths Bristol RE 1616 (LHT 173L) is captured in Weymouth. All of Smiths' Bristol REs were new to Bristol and came to Smiths via Western National, in whose livery they were operated. 12 August 1995.

Smiths Bristol RE AHT 206J is also seen on 12 August 1995.

Thamesdown Dennis Dart 114 (M114 BMR) is seen near Swindon railway station on 11 August 1995.

Thamesdown Leyland Fleetline UMR 197T is seen at Warminster on a running day, Sunday 12 September 1999.

Stagecoach Hampshire Bus Bristol VRT 442 (KRU 842W) enters Salisbury bus station (now closed) on a route run jointly with Wilts & Dorset on 29 April 1993. This bus was sadly scrapped later that year.

Southern Vectis Bristol FLF 611 (CDL 479C) and Bristol VR 665 (ODL 655R) stand at Newport bus station in August 1990. The FLF was a member of the Southern Vectis 'vintage fleet', which was why it was in Tilling Green livery. The VRT is in the livery adopted by Southern Vectis for privatisation.

Yellow Buses Dennis Dart/East Lancs 462 (M462 LLJ), seen on 31 August 2005. (Photograph copyright: Matthew Wharmby)

Yellow Buses Dennis Dart/East Lancs 475 (R475 NPR), also photographed on 31 August 2005. (Photograph copyright: Matthew Wharmby)

Yellow Buses Leyland Fleetline MFX 169W is seen resting between its peak-hours duties at Bournemouth Triangle on 13 August 2003.

Yellow Buses Leyland Fleetline 174 (MFX 174W) is seen in Christchurch on 13 August 2002.

Yellow Buses Dennis Dominator/East Lancs 266 (J266 SPR) is also seen at Bournemouth Triangle on 13 August 2003. This bus was later sold to NIBS of Essex.

Yellow Buses Dennis Dominator 268 (J268 SPR) is captured in Bournemouth on Saturday 7 August 2004. Yellow Buses' Dominators received East Lancs 'mock Alexander' bodywork.

Yellow Buses Dennis Dominator/East Lancs 261 (H261 MFX) is seen in central Bournemouth on 13 August 2003.

Yellow Buses Dennis Dominator 259 (H259 MFX) is seen leaving the vicinity of Bournemouth Triangle on the 34 to Westbourne. Behind is one of Yellow Buses' elderly Leyland Fleetlines on the 12 to Sandbanks. Saturday 30 August 2003.

Yellow Buses Volvo B7TL/East Lancs Lolyne 422 (HJ02 HFF) is seen on layover at Bournemouth Triangle on Thursday 14 August 2003.

Yellow Buses East Lancs Vyking-bodied Volvo B7TL 413 (Y413 CFX) is seen in Bournemouth on Wednesday 31 August 2005. (Photograph copyright: Matthew Wharmby)

Volvo B7TL East Lancs Myllennium HF05 HNA is seen in Bournemouth, also on 31 August 2005. (Photograph copyright: Matthew Wharmby)

Yellow Buses Wright Eclipse Gemini-bodied Volvo B7TL 184 (HF04 JWE) is pictured at Bournemouth Triangle on 31 August 2005. (Photograph copyright: Matthew Wharmby)

Yellow Buses East Lancs Vyking-bodied Volvo B7TL 426 (HF03 ODR) is caught at Bournemouth railway station, once again on 31 August 2005. (Photograph copyright: Matthew Wharmby)

Yellow Buses East Lancs Vyking-bodied Volvo B7TL 416 (Y416 CFX) is pictured in central Bournemouth. These photographs were taken while Yellow Buses was still an arm's length company owned by Bournemouth council, hence the Your Bus strapline under the Yellow Buses fleet name. 31 August 2005. (Photograph copyright: Matthew Wharmby)

Yellow Buses coach-seated East Lancs-bodied Volvo B10MD Citybus 202 (D202 ELJ) is seen in Bournemouth. This vehicle previously wore the Yellow Coaches fleetname. 31 August 2005. (Photograph copyright: Matthew Wharmby)

Although looking at first glance to be another Dennis Dominator with East Lancs 'mock Alexander' bodywork, 205 (E205 GCG) is in fact a Volvo B10M with an Alexander R Type body. It is also seen in Bournemouth on 31 August 2005. (Photograph copyright: Matthew Wharmby)

Yellow Buses 270 (T270 BPR), a Dennis Trident with an East Lancs Lolyne body, is seen in Bournemouth on 31 August 2005. (Photograph copyright: Matthew Wharmby)

A rear view of Yellow Buses 270 (T270 BPR), another Dennis Trident with an East Lancs Lolyne body, captured on the same day as above. (Photograph copyright: Matthew Wharmby)

Yellow Buses Dennis Dominator 267 (J267 SPR), seen in Bournemouth on 31 August 2005. (Photograph copyright: Matthew Wharmby)

Bristol VRT 4424 (ELJ 216V) was one of several VRTs refurbished by Wilts & Dorset. It is seen here in Bournemouth Triangle, looking very smart for a bus that is nearly quarter of a century old, on Thursday 14 August 2003.

Wilts & Dorset Bristol VRT 4448 (KRU 848W) is seen in Salisbury on 13 August 2002. This Bristol VRT is now preserved. Wilts & Dorset remained independent of any group until 2003, when they were taken over by the Go-Ahead Group.

Wilts & Dorset Bristol VRT 4432 (GEL 682V) and DAF DB250/Optare Spectra 3160 (T160 ALJ) are caught together at Salisbury bus station, also on 13 August 2002.

Wilts & Dorset Bristol VRT 4427 (ELJ 219V) is seen here on the morning of Friday 2 September 1994 in the Wiltshire market town of Devizes, about to head back to its home city of Salisbury. New to Hants & Dorset as 3427, in the early 1990s W&D's VRTs were renumbered from 3XXX to 4XXX to reflect them being considered 'low mileage' vehicles. This bus is believed to survive in Italy.

Wilts & Dorset Leyland National 3744 (EEL 894V) is captured at Salisbury bus station on Saturday 12 July 1997. The last surviving Nationals with W&D would be gone within a year.

Wilts & Dorset Bristol VR 3332 (JJT 444N) is seen in the old bus station in Amesbury on the lengthy 5 from Salisbury to Swindon. Withdrawals of native series 2 VRTs commenced in October 1992. It was maybe surprising to see that this example hadn't been renumbered into the low mileage fleet by this time, on Monday 19 April 1993.

Also seen in the old bus station in Amesbury is Wilts & Dorset Leyland Olympian A173 VFM on the 8 from Salisbury to Andover, which was operated jointly with Stagecoach Hampshire Bus. New to Crosville as DOG 173, she is seen on 19 April 1993.

When I visited Amesbury in 1997 the bus station was in the process of being rebuilt. Wilts & Dorset Optare MetroRider 2534 M534JLJ is seen in there on Saturday 12 July 1997.

Also seen in Amesbury on 12 July 1997 is Wilts & Dorset Bristol LH AFB 585V, a former Bristol Omnibus vehicle with the front cut away for use on the Sandbanks ferry. This bus was withdrawn in 2000 and is now preserved.

Two Wilts & Dorset Bristol VRTs – 4325 (JJT 437N) and 4385 (VPR 484S) – soak up the late spring sunshine in Salisbury bus station on 19 April 1993. JJT 437N is now preserved.

Wilts & Dorset Bristol VRT (JJT 441N) is looking rather scruffy when seen in Salisbury bus station on 14 May 1993.

Wilts & Dorset DAF DB250/Optare Spectra 3105 (K105 VLJ) is seen when new at Amesbury bus station on 14 May 1993.

Also seen when new is Wilts & Dorset DAF DB250 3132 (M132 HPR), photographed from the rear in Salisbury bus station in the early evening of 2 September 1994.

Wilts & Dorset Bristol VRT 4432 (GEL 682V) is seen at Salisbury bus station on 9 October 1995.

Bristol VRT 4432 (GEL 682V) is seen again some seven years later in Salisbury. It was refurbished by Wilts & Dorset in 1999, the most obvious external sign of this being the replacement of several windows with non-opening ones. 13 August 2002.

Wilts & Dorset Optare MetroRider 2523 (K523 UJT) is seen at Amesbury bus station on 24 November 1994.

Wilts & Dorset Optare MetroRider P235 CTV is fully loaded as it leaves Salisbury on the limited-stop interurban X7 to Southampton on 13 August 2002.

Wilts & Dorset Optare Solo S629 JRU is seen entering the new Amesbury bus station on 14 January 2002. This bus saw further use with Centerbus.

Also at Amesbury bus station is Wilts & Dorset Optare MetroRider 2524 (K524 UJT).

Above and below: Wilts & Dorset Bristol VRT 4448 (KRU 848W) is seen in two views at Amesbury bus station on 14 January 2002. This bus is now preserved.

Wilts & Dorset coach-seated Leyland Olympian 3904 (A904 JPR) is seen in Poole bus station waiting to head back on the lengthy X3 to Salisbury. The coach seats made this bus very suitable for that route. It is in the dual-purpose version of W&D livery. This bus was later re-seated with bus seats and received the standard bus livery. 29 April 1993.

Wilts & Dorset DAF DB250/Optare Spectra 3136 (M136 KRU), wearing dual-purpose livery, enters Amesbury bus station on 14 January 2002.

Wilts & Dorset Optare Solo S632 JRU is seen here on Fisherton Street in Salisbury, also on 14 January 2002.

Wilts & Dorset Bristol VRT GEL 682V is seen in Salisbury city centre on 14 January 2002. This bus is believed to survive in the ownership of a junior school in Norwich.

Wilts & Dorset DAF DB250/Optare Spectra M133 HPR is also captured at Salisbury bus station on Monday 14 January 2002.

Wilts & Dorset Optare Solo 2620 (R620 NFX) is captured standing at Salisbury bus station on 13 August 2002.

Wilts & Dorset DAF DB250/Optare Spectra 3127 (L127 ELJ) is caught here basking in the morning sunshine in Lymington bus station on 4 July 2007.

Wilts & Dorset Bristol VRT 4417 (UDL 674S), new to Southern Vectis, is seen in Bournemouth on 7 August 2004. Bristol VRTs had long lives with W&D. It is interesting to note that the passenger doors on this bus are from a series 2, as can be seen by the cream window rubbers.

Wilts & Dorset was taken over by the Go-Ahead Group in August 2003 and the company's new owners rebranded some services in the Poole/Bournemouth area as More. Volvo B7RLE 112 (HF54 HGC) is seen here on 31 August 2005. (Photograph copyright: Matthew Wharmby)

Volvo B7RLE 113 (HF54 HGD) is seen in Bournemouth on 31 August 2005. (Photograph copyright: Matthew Wharmby)

Wilts & Dorset Optare Solo 2653 (V652 DFX) awaits passengers in Bournemouth on 31 August 2005. (Photograph copyright: Matthew Wharmby)

Wilts & Dorset Optare Solo 2657 (V657 DFX) stands in Bournemouth on the same day in the new livery introduced by W&D's new owners. (Photograph copyright: Matthew Wharmby)

Wilts & Dorset DAF DB250/Optare Spectra 3172 (Y172 FEL), with route branding for the X3 Bournemouth Triangle, is caught on 30 August 2003.

Saturday 30 August 2003 was a very warm, sunny day. However, Wilts & Dorset convertible Leyland Olympian 4907 (A990 XAF) is seen wearing its roof when captured at Bournemouth Triangle.

By 2005 it was getting very difficult to find Bristol VRTs in normal service. However, 31 August 2005 saw Wilts & Dorset 4427 (ELJ 219V) on a local service in Bournemouth. Some of W&D's VRTs would remain in service until 2007. (Photograph copyright: Matthew Wharmby)

Wilts & Dorset Optare Solo 2601 (R601 NFX) stands in Bournemouth on 8 March 2001 while working to Poole.

Wilts & Dorset Optare Excel 3602 (W602 PLJ) is photographed in Wimborne Minster on 10 August 2004 ...

...while Wilts & Dorset Optare Excel 3604 (W604 PLJ) is seen at Bournemouth Triangle on 8 March 2001.

Wilts & Dorset Bristol VRT 4432 (GEL 682V) makes another appearance, this time basking in the sunlight in Poole bus station on 30 August 2003.

GEL 682V makes its final appearance in the book, this time photographed at lunchtime on Monday 9 August 2004 with a 1965 Ford Anglia behind it.

While not the best of photographs due to the poor light, I consider this image worth including, as it is the only photograph I have of any Wilts & Dorset DAF SB220/Optare Deltas. 3502 and 3505 are seen at Poole bus station on Saturday 30 August 2003.

Wilts & Dorset Bristol VRT 4426 (ELJ 218V) is seen on Monday 1 September 2003.

Wilts & Dorset UDL 674S makes another appearance in this book, its appearance belying its age. New to Southern Vectis as 674 in 1978, it is seen here in Bournemouth when twenty-six years old, on 7 August 2004.

Wilts & Dorset DAF DB250/Northern Counties Palatine 2 3157 (M645 RCP) is seen at Swanage on Saturday 30 August 2003. New to Abus of Bristol, she was converted to convertible open top and the suspension was later modified for the Sandbanks Ferry.

Above and below: I've decided to finish the book with a couple of rear views. Above, Wilts & Dorset Bristol VRT 4424 (ELJ 216V) is seen at Ringwood on 24 April 2002, while below 3418 (UDL 675S) and 3435 (GEL 685V) are seen in the late afternoon sunshine of 19 April 1993 at Lymington bus station.